The Es
Solution Focused
Practice

Andrew Gibson

The Essence of Solution Focused Practice

Copyright © Andrew Gibson 2025

PRINT ISBN 978-1-916776-68-5
DIGITAL ISBN 978-1-916776-69-2

Published by Fisher King Publishing
www.fisherkingpublishing.co.uk

This book is dedicated to
Dr John Williams.

'If you aim for the stars, you
might reach the top of the
stairs.'

May this book help you find your
first steps on many long
and fruitful journeys.

Reviews...

"I am very happy you have written this little book with the essence of SF. The world needs it! I am looking forward to holding the book in my hands and sharing it with the world."
Dr. Petra Müller-Demary - *Founder, Solutionsurfers, Romania*

"I love your book. The simplicity is stunning! Everybody who will read and look at the book will capture the essence of SF. It will help more than many written pages and powerpoint presentations. I'm looking forward to holding a copy with dedication in my hands when we next meet. And of course, I will recommend it to my clients!"
Julia Kalenberg - *Solutions Focused Trainer, Coach and Keynote Speaker, Switzerland*

"What a wonderful resource and so inspirational. Really got me thinking."
Sam Matthews - *Head of Delivery, Pilotlight Charity, UK*

"It is a pleasure to read and look at your book and I really like how you turn complex things into wonderful simplicity. Looking forward to being able to recommend and show 'The Essence of SFP' to colleagues, clients and students."
Carola Baxmann - *Founder and Owner, Gelöst! Akademie, Germany*

"I truly enjoyed reading it. It's a concise, powerful, and to-the-point piece of work. The content is very accessible, and the message is communicated clearly."
Liselotte Pattyn - *Solution Focused Therapist and Coach, Belgium*

"The book is BRILLIANT!! I can use it right away in my team."
Liselotte Baeijaert - *Founder, ilfaro BV, Belgium, and Land aan Zee Centre, The Netherlands*

1

Notes

We have a problem

Notes

It blocks our view of what we want.

Notes

If we talk about our problem, it grows.

Notes

If we talk about what we want instead,
this is Common Sense

2

Notes

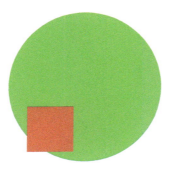

When we describe what we want,
we think of other people, and other
resources. Maybe they can help?

Notes

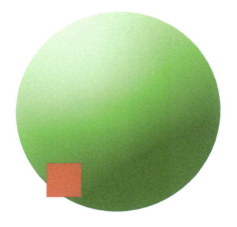

Our network of family, friends and acquaintances is a resource that can help us progress towards what we want.

This is our Social Capital.

Notes

3

Notes

What do you want to do?

This is a very common question,
especially when we have a problem.

What do you want to do?

After we do something about the problem, we often don't get what we want.

We have created new problems. We use more time and resources when we tackle them.

If we want to do different things, the problem grows.

What do you want? ~~to do~~

If we start by describing what we want, this will help us before we act.

The richer we make the description, the easier it is to compare possible next steps and then choose one.

When we act, we will know what to look for to tell us our chosen action is working.

Notes

4

Notes

Realising what we want takes time,
and many steps.

Notes

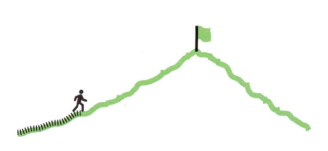

As we take steps and notice signs
of what we want, we know we are
progressing towards it.

If we notice no signs of what we want,
we stop. We check again what we want,
and we notice our progress.

Then, we take new steps towards
what we want.

(We do not go back to the start!)

Notes

M	T	W	Th	F	S	S
		1	2	3	4	5
6	7	8	9	10	11	12
13	14	15	16	17	18	19
20	21	22	23	24	25	26
27	28	29	30	31		

Making progress takes time.
We use time in our conversations.

M	T	W	Th	F	S	S
		1	2	3	4	5
6	7	8	9	10	11	12
13	14	15	16	17	18	19
20	21	22	23	24	25	26
27	28	29	30	31		

When we accept that reaching what we
want takes time, our journey of small
steps is easier to describe.
We use a three-stage process.

Notes

First, we describe our perfect future.

Notes

Then, we seek some of our perfect future
happening now or in the past.

Finally, we imagine a short time into the future. We describe what we would notice if we were on the path to what we want.

Notes

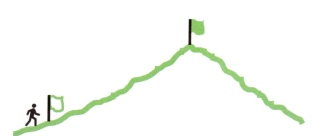

Only then do we take our first step.

Notes

$$1+2+3+4$$

Notes

1

When stuck with a problem, focus
on what is wanted instead.

What will you notice when you
have what you want?

What else?

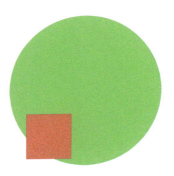

Notes

2

Explore what your network
will notice.

What will they notice when you
have what you want?

What else?

3

What do you want? ~~to do~~

Always spend time exploring and describing what you want before you decide what to do.

The richer the description you create, the easier it is to choose your next steps.

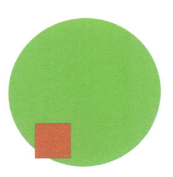

4

It takes time and many steps to reach what you want.

Include time in your conversation.

We time travel to the future, then the present, and recent past. We find resources to help us with the next steps towards our perfect future.

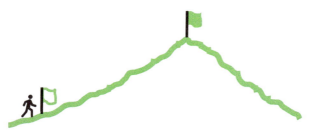

Notes

1 Common Sense

2 Social Capital

3 Description before Action

4 Time

Combined, these are:

The Essence of
Solution Focused Practice

An Example

You arrive at the station, and you hail a taxi. The driver asks, 'Where do you want to go?'

You reply, 'Please take me away from here.'

The driver would repeat, 'Where do you want to go?'

If you insisted on them 'taking you away from here,' the next question would likely be, 'How much money have you got?'

They would then drive you away from the station until your money was spent and leave you somewhere that was indeed 'away from' the station.

You have 'solved your problem,' but have you got what you wanted?

It is common sense to work out where you want to go before you get into the taxi. Indeed, by knowing where you want to go, you will have made a positive choice that the taxi is the best transport to your destination compared to other options.

When you are on your journey, external change happens all the time.

The driver uses their local knowledge to avoid traffic jams and roadworks. Satellite navigation presents them with options regularly throughout the journey. When a better route is available, the driver changes course, and you continue towards your destination. As you make progress, both the driver and the sat-nav regularly check that the taxi is following the optimum route.

We use this destination focused, step-by-step approach in daily life. It is the natural, common-sense way to make progress and to get what you want.

Like the taxi driver, we all have skills, tools, and experience. We bring these to every occasion and conversation. I hope that the Essence of Solution Focused Practice enhances your skills, tools, and experience, whatever they are, and wherever you employ them.

Acknowledgments

This book took one hour, eighteen years to write.

I am grateful to all my friends and mentors in the Solution Focused Practice community. This work would not exist without their help and guidance.

This was written in the garden of Land aan Zee, Burgh Hamsteede, The Netherlands on Sunday 18th May, 2025. (https://landaanzee. org/en/)

I am grateful to Liselotte, Petra, Carola, Christoph and Julia for their spontaneous support, and to John, Annie, Eva, Liselotte and Michiel for co-creating the opportunity.

My introduction to Solution Focused Practice in 2007 was thanks to my dear friend Greg, may he rest in peace. I am grateful to Chris, Mark, Paul Z, John, Steve, Anton, Kirsten, Peter, Jenny, Dion, Jason and countless others for their help, guidance and support these last eighteen years.

I must also thank all the trainees and my clients at SW Yorkshire NHS Trust where this model has been thoroughly tested since my first training course there in 2015. It is an honour to support you all. Specific thanks to Carmain, and to Nick, Vafa and Malcolm for their help and support.

I live in Leeds, Yorkshire, UK with my family, Natalie, Alex and Banjo (our dog). Thank you, Natalie for your editing and advice, as well as your love, patience and support.

Andrew Gibson

Resources

To purchase multiple copies of this book, please contact Rachel at rt@fisherkingpublishing.co:uk

You will find additional resources, including my SFP Coaching Skills video training course based on the Essence of Solution Focused Practice at https://solutionfocusedonline.co.uk/home

The model shared here is discussed in Episode 2 of the 'Toward Solutions Podcast,' available via podcast providers.

To connect with the author, please go to https://andrew-gibson.com

For more resources and information, please see the Journal of Solution Focused Practice https://journalsfp.org/

You will find my friends and colleagues bringing Solution Focused Practice to organisations at SOLWorld http://solworld.org/ and at SF in Organisations https://www.sfio.org/

Andrew Gibson

Andrew Gibson first encountered Solution Focused Practice in 2007. Working as an Enterprise Coach in Bradford, he was lucky enough to meet Greg Vinnicombe and start his SFP journey.

With Greg, Andrew learned and co-trained SFP to large teams of Social Workers (Hartlepool), NHS Child and Adolescent Mental Health Practitioners (SW Yorkshire NHS Trust, Wakefield), and Enterprise Coaches (Bradford). Tragically, Greg was killed in 2015 while on holiday. His legacy lives on in the work that Andrew does, and through the training company Greg set up with his friend John Wheeler, https://www.solutionfocused.training/.

Andrew's specialism is helping people who help people. With that mission in mind, he:

helps charities/non-profits find sustainable revenue from their activities;

helps people with next to nothing explore their new business ideas;

helps create economic growth in communities;

improves productivity, and at the same time improves morale and team spirit in small and large organisations;

helps people and organisations create and share useful stories in their networks, harnessing their social capital;

loves helping with 'impossible' challenges, especially when people are 'stuck'.

He trains SFP Coaching Skills in Organisations and tailors his programmes around the Essence of SFP.

He is the author of two books which bring SFP to specific applications. 'What's Your URP? (2019) and 'Make Life Simple' (2020), available online.

He contributes to the SFP Community as a regular conference speaker and keynote. He is Chair (Operations) of the Journal of SFP.

He is always happy to help, and you can contact him via info@businessservicesleeds.co.uk